Dedicated to the escape of Emma's first baby tooth.

Filipino Folk Dances

There are as many Folk Dances as there are cultures in the Philippines.

Folk dances are how our ancestors reach through time to tell us their stories. Imagine a dance from the southern tip of the islands depicting an epic of a forgotten Prince in bold colors. From the north, a mountain tribe depics the daily ritual of collecting water in their red tribal clothes and beads. Another dance shows a courtship of two lovers in clothes inspired by the fashion from Spain.

Each dance is different and as diverse as the people who inhabit the Philippines. This book does not depict all the dances from the archipelago as no book could possibly contain them all, but this highlights some of the most recognizable folk dances that are still performed today.

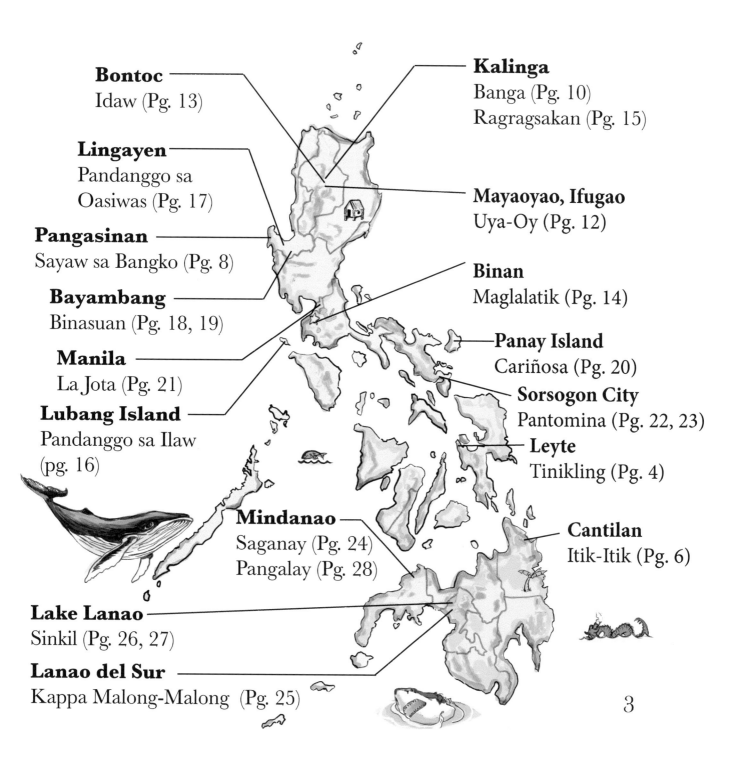

Bontoc
Idaw (Pg. 13)

Kalinga
Banga (Pg. 10)
Ragragsakan (Pg. 15)

Lingayen
Pandanggo sa
Oasiwas (Pg. 17)

Mayaoyao, Ifugao
Uya-Oy (Pg. 12)

Pangasinan
Sayaw sa Bangko (Pg. 8)

Bayambang
Binasuan (Pg. 18, 19)

Binan
Maglalatik (Pg. 14)

Manila
La Jota (Pg. 21)

Panay Island
Cariñosa (Pg. 20)

Sorsogon City
Pantomina (Pg. 22, 23)

Lubang Island
Pandanggo sa Ilaw
(pg. 16)

Leyte
Tinikling (Pg. 4)

Mindanao
Saganay (Pg. 24)
Pangalay (Pg. 28)

Cantilan
Itik-Itik (Pg. 6)

Lake Lanao
Sinkil (Pg. 26, 27)

Lanao del Sur
Kappa Malong-Malong (Pg. 25)

3

4

Tinikling

Leyte, Visayas. This dance is known as the national dance of the Philippines. It originated in the 1500s in Leyte, an island in the Visaya.

The dance imitates the movement of tikling birds as they walk between grass stems, run over tree branches, or dodge bamboo traps set by rice farmers.

The dance involves two people beating and sliding two bamboo poles on the ground and against each other as one or more dancers step over and between them. The rhythm starts slow, and often becomes more complicated and intricate.

A tikling bird

Itik-Itik

Cantilan, Surigao del Sur. Itik-Itik, or the Duck Dance, imitates the movements of the bird it is named after. The steps are short, and hand gestures imitate the movement of a bird's wings.

Popular folklore states that the dance was created by a maiden dancer in Surigao del Norte. While at a baptism, she was asked to dance and improvised these steps.

This dance is typically performed by young girls in simple provincial dresses, often in yellow, with matching headbands.

6

Sayaw Sa Bangko

Pangasinan Province. Literally translates to "dance on a bench", which is often performed at fiestas and is a lively crowd pleaser.

It is performed by a couple on a narrow bench, inching and hopping from one end to another. Dancers show skill in staying up on the bench As they exchange places by stepping around each other, or helping each other "jump" over benches. Sometimes multipe benches will be placed on top of each other to add height and complication.

Banga

Kalinga Mountain Province. The word "banga" simply means "jar". It is an clay container used for several household necessities such as cooking, holding water, and food storage.

The dance originates from the Kalinga villages, an area rich with rice terraces. It was inspired by the daily practice of women stacking these pots on their head to collect water. The women's grace, posture and balance moves to the rhythm of gangsa wind chimes. Many girls may put all of their pots on one girl's head, stacking it high during the climax of the song.

10

11

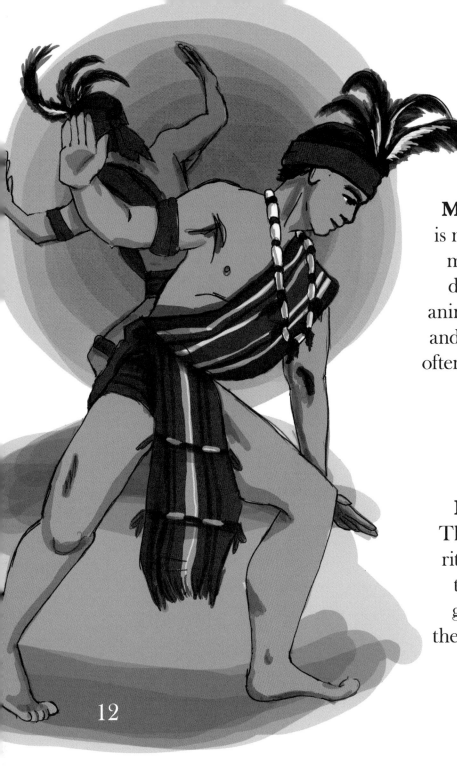

Uya-Oy (Left)

Mayaoyao, Ifugao. This dance is mostly performed at weddings by members of the Ifugao tribe. The dance mimics the mighty hunting animals, such as the Sakpaya Hawk, and is set to the music of gongs. It is often danced by affluent members to highlight their influence.

Idaw (Right)

Bontoc Mountain Province. This dance often depicts a hunting ritual or battle performed before a tribal war. The tribes men would go out and look up and watch for the scared Idaw bird. Which is said to lead the tribe to victory.

Maglalatik

Binan, Laguna Province.
Also known as Manlalatik, or Magbabao. It is performed mostly by men. Coconut halves are attached to the man's torso and legs. The dance is performed by banging the coconut halves together to the rhythm of a fast drum beat.

Elements of the dance have the fundamentals of boxing and trapping, with movements taken from Filipino Martial Arts.

14

Ragragsakan

Kalinga Province. The word "ragragsakan" is an Ilocano word meaning "merriment". The ragragsakan dance was inspired by Kalinga maidens balancing labba baskets on their heads as they carry the things people need durings fiestas. The dance features red scarves worn about the shoulders or in the basket as the dancers sing.

15

Pandanggo sa ilaw (Left)

Lubang Island, Mindoro. Known as the "Dance of the Lights". Each locality has their own version of this dance, but each one is lively with typically three candle lights, usually in a small glass container, that the dancers must balance and is normally accompanied by lively clapping.

Pandanggo sa Oasiwas (Right)

Lingayen, Pangasinan. This version of the Light dance comes from the fishing towns of Lingayen in Pangasinan. "Oasiwas" means "swing", and the lights would be placed in a napkin or hook and be swung by the dancers to upbeat music as part of a celebration.

17

18

Binasuan

Bayambang, Pangasinan. Binasuan is a folk dance that originated in Bayambang, Pangasinan. The word "binasuan" means "with the use of drinking glasses." Similar to Pandanggo sa Ilaw and Pandanggo sa Oasawis, it is performed with cups balanced on the hands and the top of the head. Instead of candles, the cups contain a type of rice wine, and is performed during weddings and other fiestas.

19

Cariñosa

Panay Island. The word means "loving " or "affectionate one". It is a romantic and flirtatious dance with couples at the center. The style and music is heavily influenced by the Spanish, who occupied the Philippines from the 15th to the 19th century.

The typical costume for this dance is the Maria Clara, and Barong Tagalog. Fans and handkerchiefs play an important role in the choreography.

20

La Jota

There are many dances influenced by Jota originating from Aragon, Spain. The popular versions include La Jota Mocadena, La Jota Manilena, and A La Jota.

The dances comprise of heavy Spanish influences with Filipino traditional footsteps. Some incorporate local instruments. The costumes for these dances are a dress called the Maria Clara, a traditional Filipino dress with iconic butterfly sleeves for women, and the barong Tagalog, a light, thin white shirt with a high collar for men.

Pantomina

Sorsogon City, Sorsogon Province. This is a courtship dance, and is meant to pantomime the courtship of doves. This dance is tradionally performed during wedding festivities by the couple and their visitors. The dance is still popular in the Bicol Region.

The pantomina was featured in Francisca Reyes Aquino's first-ever folk dance book, Philippine Folk Dances and Games, published in February 1926. The dance, according to Aquino, was also called Salampati during the Spanish occupation.

Sagayan

Mindanao. The Maranao and Maguindanao tribes use this dance to depict Prince Bantugan, the handsomer, younger brother of the envious King of Bumbaran. When enemies attacked the Kingdom, the good Prince raised armaments and went to defend his country. This dance depicts his raising of troops and his victory in battle. The dancer is depicted with colorful armor and clothes, a sword, shield and noise-makers.

24

Kappa Malong-Malong

Lanao del Sur, Mindanao Province.
The dance is sometimes known as "Sambi sa Malong", and originates from Mindanao.

The dance simply shows the various ways to wear a Malong, which is a tubular piece of cloth. It's similar to a sarong which is worn in Malaysia. The dance can involve both men and women.

25

Singkil

Lake Lanao, Mindanao.
This is a dance of a Princess, and is the traditional dance of the Maranao people in Southern Philippines. The dance features a Princess and her handmaiden, as well as a Prince. It is performed similarly to Tinikling, where two couples rhythmically tap bamboo poles which the main dancers step around.

The dance depicts the story of a princess who guided by a troupe of spirit guides who protect her from a prince with a roving eye. She dances through the bamboo, symbollic of the earth quaking, as many females dance with fans, symbolizing a strong wind.

26

Pangalay

Mindanao. The Tausug people of Sulu perform this "fingernail" dance. It is similar to Balinese and Thai dances. The dance's origins are traced to before Christianity and Islam arrived to the Philippines. It is based on the Buddhist concept of male and female celestial angels.

The dance features movements that are more similar to folk dances from the Asian mainland.

The End.

When Tita KitKat attempted to buy Filipino themed books for her preschool nephew, she found that there weren't many out there. As an overbearing Filipino Aunty, she decided that her nephews and nieces would have books that taught them about this half of their heritage, even if she has to make them herself.

Instagram: Tita.KitKat
Facebook: TitaKitKatOfficial
Web: www.TitaKitKat.com

Printed in Great Britain
by Amazon